For Jason Miranda —

Warmly,

Maria Ldl...

Strategic Marketing
Insights on Setting Smart Directions for Your Business

W9-BHB-879

Strategic Marketing: Insights on Setting Smart Directions for Your Business
by Marcia Yudkin

Copyright © 2010 by Marcia Yudkin

Publisher: Creative Ways Publishing
               PO Box 305
               Goshen, MA 01032
               www.marketinginsightguides.com

Cover Design and Interior Design: Kitty Werner, RSBPress

Cover Photo: © Wong Sze Fei/Fotolia.com

Author Photo: Gila Yudkin

ISBN 978-0-9716407-3-3

Printed in the United States of America

Strategic Marketing

Insights on Setting Smart Directions for Your Business

Marcia Yudkin

Marketing Insight Guides
Creative Ways Publishing

Introduction

As I was organizing the chapters of this book, an email arrived from someone who said he'd been receiving my newsletter for about three years, and the time had come to hire me. When was I available for a chat about what he needed?

The same week, I advised a client who wants to build his national reputation as a medical expert that displaying little Google ads at his web site would make him seem either unsuccessful or greedy. He agreed with me that with the reputation, the higher fees and exciting opportunities he was seeking would in the long run offset the near-term loss of ad income.

These two incidents illustrate the challenges and payoffs of marketing strategy. When you set strategy for yourself or your organization, you take actions that may provide little immediate evidence that they're working, yet nevertheless they eventually bring you the kind of business success you wanted.

In this book, you learn the importance of planning for what you want *and* don't want to do and have in your business. Your reward: clients you enjoy, fees that handsomely reward you and energy left over to appreciate the non-business side of your life.

Discover too the dynamics of familiarity and trust, the principles of profit and a toolkit of marketing methods that re-engineer a trickle of sales into a torrent.

The lessons apply whether you're a wishing-was-busier solo practitioner, the harried owner of a mid-sized business or a seat-of-your-pants marketer at a sizable organization.

These chapters originate in a weekly column, *The Marketing Minute*, that I've published since 1998. You can sign up for a subscription at www.yudkin.com/markmin.htm. It's free. I've added action steps to deepen your understanding of the principles involved and how to apply them.

Contents

Part 1
Shaping Your Business

Put Aside Commodity Fears

Coming to a mall near you, perhaps: a franchise charging one-third of your professional service fees.

To many service providers, this scenario gets their hearts pounding with fear. When cut-rate competitors appear, they feel their livelihood is in jeopardy. Is it?

According to an Associated Press story, traditional massage therapists have little reason to fear as a franchise called Massage Envy opens storefronts in malls offering no-frills therapeutic massages for a low monthly fee.

Nearly a quarter of Massage Envy's customers had never before had a paid massage. In this way, the franchise is actually increasing the overall market for the service, noted the article, quoting a customer who would never have ventured into a swanky day spa or traditional massage therapy studio.

Likewise, the very existence of low-cost providers helps reposition massage as an affordable indulgence rather than a luxury, encouraging more frequent usage.

Massage therapists who can demonstrate their greater experience or specialty skills (massage for athletes, pregnant women, accident victims, etc.) can most easily maintain their fees in the face of mall-ization.

~ ~

Action Steps

✦ In two columns on a sheet of paper, list all the advantages and disadvantages of buying what you sell from a commodity provider. Highlight two or more of the disadvantages on the list and adopt those factors as your differentiators so your ideal customers overlook or even enjoy your higher prices.

✦ Examine your marketing copy in the light of this question: Is it crystal clear how you differ from low-priced competition? If not, revamp how you describe your company so you highlight what buyers can't get from the dime-a-dozen crowd.

Commodity? No, Opportunity

It's become a commodity–you can't charge what you used to."

I've heard this lament countless times, usually in a glum, helpless tone of voice followed by, "I guess it's time to change careers."

If you feel that people shop only by price for what you sell and regard suppliers as interchangeable, look again. Almost always, you'll see deficiencies in the way the commodity is packaged and delivered. And those point toward opportunities to serve ignored needs and rise above the slide toward ever-lower rates.

For instance, the AARP organization chewed out the cell-phone industry for making devices that are too small for folks over 50 to use and offering incomprehensible contracts and too many "dead zone" surprises. The company that develops a senior-friendly product and service can quickly set itself apart from competitors.

Likewise, web hosting companies escape commodity status by offering more hand-holding, more business advice or specialization in a certain industry or type of site.

Decide not to try to be all things to all people and you're on the road out of Commodity City.

Action Steps

✦ List at least three types of customers you would rather not please. When you subtract those groups from your customer base, who remains and what do they value? Rewrite your marketing copy so your non-customers understand you're not for them and the others know how you match their preferences.

✦ Think about the restaurants you like best, stores you go way out of your way to visit, books you happily get on waiting lists for at the library and the car mechanic you treasure. What lifts those items out of commodity status for you? Do you detect any clues you can use in differentiating what you sell and how you do business?

What About Average Joe and Jane?

Many business coaches discourage marketers from targeting niches where the average individual or organization can't afford moderate to high fees.

For many service providers, this consideration is not relevant.

The reigning question should instead be: Are there enough potential clients who *are* willing to pay your fees?

You may need only a small number of clients per year to keep your schedule full, and the niche contains thousands of ideal clients. Then forget about the others, and market to those you want to attract.

This logic (backed by research and observation) makes numerous seemingly ill-chosen niches quite viable.

For instance, according to conventional wisdom, aspiring painters and sculptors are "starving artists." Typically that may be true. So what? Many Baby Boomers who succeeded in another career now want to develop their artistic talents and are willing to invest in services that help them develop into a successful artist.

Likewise, while the typical nonprofit organization may be struggling, tens of thousands easily pay prevailing rates for everything.

Unless you're aiming to dominate your marketplace, don't give Average Joe and Jane too much thought!

Action Steps

+ Calculate how many customers you need per year to meet your income goals. Then research the size of your potential customer universe. Divide the first number by the second number to arrive at the percentage of potential customers you need to attract. Does that ratio indicate that you need to scramble or that you can afford to be selective?

+ Create three or more detailed portraits of individual customers who differ greatly from Average Joe and Jane and might be delighted to buy from you. Now think about how you can adjust your marketing pitch or offerings so as to attract those people.

Avoid the Dismal Middle

In the runup to Christmas 2003, luxury retailers did very well, discount stores did fine and establishments with ordinary pricing suffered. This trend actually applies to all kinds of businesses, according to Adrian Slywotzky and David Morrison, authors of *Profit Patterns: 30 Ways to Anticipate and Profit from Strategic Forces Reshaping Your Business.*

"Being caught in 'the middle' is a lousy place to be, strategically," they say. "The increasing sophistication of the global business community has, in most markets, punished 'the middle' unmercifully."

People looking for unusual or customized solutions are usually willing to pay more, while people shopping by price normally select the least expensive option. You may pride yourself in having a quality product or service at an acceptable price, but this isn't a smart survival strategy unless you can also cite powerful differences between you and competitors. And if you have compelling advantages to offer, why not build yourself into an exclusive brand?

You can't simply raise prices. You need also to add value— or do a knockout job of selling the extra value you've been providing all along.

Action Steps

+ Think of one or more exclusive purveyors in your industry, one or more middle-of-the-roaders and one or more discounters. Next, consider what you'd have to add or subtract from how you operate to join each of those groups. If this brings on any blinding insights, get busy implementing what you realized.

+ List all of your objections to moving out of the dismal middle positioning. Place a star next to the objections that feel toughest to overcome. Now think hard about businesses that transcend those objections. What can you learn from them?

Mr. Bean's Business Philosophy

The other day, I had occasion to look up the L.L. Bean guarantee and was fascinated to find the text of the notice Mr. Bean himself hung on the wall of his Maine outdoorware store in 1916:

> I do not consider a sale complete until goods are worn out and customer still satisfied.

This wowed me. It has so much more depth than the store's current slogan, "Guaranteed. You Have Our Word."

Mr. Bean's credo contains these elements:

+ Care about craftsmanship. Things generally don't get used to the point of being worn out unless they are well made.

+ Long-range perspective. He can't possibly be aiming for a quick buck when the outcome of a transaction hangs in the balance for years and years.

✦ The customer decides. He didn't present himself as the arbiter of quality. It's clearly up to the customer to use his or her own criteria to decide whether or not their purchase was satisfactory.

Even if you sell intangible knowledge, you can follow his lead by delivering long-term value in the eyes of clients.

On the Web

Read the 33 fascinating replies I received when I asked *Marketing Minute* subscribers whether they had a business philosophy:

www.yudkin.com/philosophy.htm

Building a Non-Local Clientele

Despite a slow economy and having recently moved to a town of some 920 people, 2004 was my best year up to that point. Just one 2004 client lived within 40 miles of me, and even in that case, we worked together by email and telephone.

What does it take to provide high-level services to clients you never meet face to face? Building a reputation is the secret. While this works fastest within a narrow niche, these strategies help you build a reputation without limiting yourself to a small niche:

+ A newsletter (like *The Marketing Minute*) that people read and pass along
+ Media coverage in magazines and web sites read by your ideal clients
+ A content-rich web site that attracts people searching for information and resources

- ✦ Published articles (better: books) that evoke "Gosh, this person is the perfect one to help us" in readers
- ✦ Referrals and repeat business from satisfied clients
- ✦ Specific, tangible results referenced in the above

Some of these strategies also enable you to create a portable business, where money keeps flowing in while you travel—this month Hawaii, next month the south of France.

On the Web

When I celebrated the 25-year anniversary of my business, I held a teleseminar explaining the process of transforming a local business to a virtual one. Normally the recording of this teleseminar costs $37, but receive it free by inserting the coupon code STRATEGY in the shopping cart when you place your order at:

www.yudkin.com/virtual.htm

Why Mentoring Produces Focus

Many business and personal coaches highlight accountability as the #1 benefit of engaging them. The coach expects the client to carry out commitments, and that expectation helps results to come into being.

I agree: This process works. There's another dynamic I've seen in motion that fewer coaches talk about.

Without a mentor, some people careen from one conflicting method or claim to another, wasting time and energy on theory instead of action. A mentor who has achieved what the client hopes to do can steer the client past "Who is right?" dilemmas to tasks and accomplishments.

Get a mentor's in-the-know direction if you're swamped in Hamlet-like indecision and opinion overload. Just make sure the mentor:

- ✦ respects your goals
- ✦ sets challenges

- points out your weaknesses and blind spots
- offers options rather than a formula
- encourages you to persevere

Stop stewing and wondering. Find a mentor and move forward!

Action Steps

- Increasingly, veteran consultants and authors hang out a shingle to mentor those less experienced in their industry or occupation. Ask around at conferences or do a web search to learn who has a mentoring program. Before signing up, read everything you can find by them to determine whether or not they're a match for your personality, values and goals.

- Often you can talk someone who doesn't have a mentoring program into starting one. If you find someone you'd like to learn from, tell them why you'd like to become their mentoree, how you imagine the arrangement working, what you'd be willing to pay and how they would benefit. Make a strong case, and it's likely they'll agree to your proposal.

Part 2
Choosing Clients

Pursue Your Ideal Clients

When I coach marketing consultants-to-be about targeting their consulting practice, I ask, "What kinds of people and companies do you enjoy and not enjoy working with?" It's a vital question, and I've long believed that success comes sooner when you like your clients.

According to David Maister, author of *True Professionalism* and *The Trusted Advisor,* only about 20 percent of professionals love their clients, 60-70 percent tolerate them and 10-20 percent can't stand them. The figures of how many enjoy their work are the same. Asked whether or not they think clients can tell, nearly everyone concedes that yep, the clients know.

Maister says it's as if the majority are operating with the mission statement, "We won't screw up, but we're nothing special."

Are you putting up with a gray haze of indifference or outright contempt between you and those you serve? Identify your favorite clients, analyze what they have in common, and in a disciplined way, seek more like them. With more conscious marketing, you can gradually steer your practice into the zone where you cherish those you work for.

Action Steps

+ On one page, answer the question, "What kinds of clients do you most enjoy working with?" On another page, address "What kinds of clients are most profitable for you?" Look for commonalities in your answers to the two questions, and regear your marketing toward that psychologically and financially profitable intersection. If you find no such intersection, still steer your efforts toward attracting clients you like and watch your productivity and morale improve.

+ Score yourself on how often you work with clients you can't stand: Very often (0), sometimes (1), once in a while (2) or never (3). Decide on two actions you can take to terminate, turn down or refer away your annoyers. Three months and six months later, score yourself again. Did your number go up?

Attracting the Wrong Crowd?

Although occasionally someone approaches me wanting to understand why clients they'd rather not have keep showing up, more often I see people just silently suffering the effects of this situation:

+ Communication difficulties with clients. Do you see lots of misunderstandings where you say something and they miss the point or vice versa? Feel like you're not speaking the same language?

+ You're thinking about tossing in the towel. Revenue is OK, but you feel stressed and unhappy day after day as you carry on business.

+ Customers wanting their money back. If you provide good quality, a problematical rate of refund requests could indicate a mismatch with customers' expectations. It may be easier to attract those with expectations better matched to your business than to combat mismatched thinking.

✦ Growth is stagnant or slipping. You get few complaints, but no raving enthusiasm. Serve your perfect customers, and natural growth occurs from referrals and repeat business.

Attract the customers you feel best about serving, and everyone benefits. You easily get along with one another, they love your services and products, and your bean counters smile along with you.

On the Web

Read replies from a *Marketing Minute* subscriber survey on the most prevalent kinds of troublesome clients and strategies respondents have used to reduce their numbers and impact:

www.marketingformore.com/survey2.htm

I need to set processes & develop more people — The relationship is stagnant they don't really seem to work w/ the junior people, & get passed or

Identify Futile Efforts

If you've ever wailed "Why don't they get it?" because people who clearly need your services don't flock to buy, try this typology on for size.

Group 1: They have a problem but do not realize they have a problem.

Group 2: They realize they have a problem but understand it very differently than you do. For example, you'd diagnose a midlife crisis, but they consider their anguish and wild behavior a marital problem or career dilemma.

Group 3: They know they have a problem and understand it roughly as you would but call it something else.

Group 4: They know they have a problem and understand and name it as you do.

Members of Group 4 are the easiest to get in the door as clients. Group 3 are also easily snagged as long as you discover and use their words.

Group 2 require more imaginative educational outreach, as they are looking for a different sort of solution or tool than you offer.

Stop trying to reach Group 1, the oblivious, as they will never seek you out or respond to your marketing.

Action Steps

+ To reach Group 3, convene four to eight members of the audience you're trying to sell to and ask them open-ended questions that get them talking about the problem you solve. Record the session and while listening, identify the terminology they use to describe that problem. Repeat with another group if necessary. Incorporate their language into your headlines and marketing pitches.

+ To reach Group 2, place articles in magazines and newsletters they read, arrange speaking engagements that educate a captive audience on your perspective and ask influencers who understand the problem as you do to refer people to you who need your solution.

Slim Down Your Client List

It seems logical that if you want revenues to rise, you need more customers. According to a study by John Bowen of CEG Worldwide, however, the opposite may be true.

Of more than 700 financial advisors in the study, those earning less than $75,000 a year had an average of 201 clients, those earning $75,000-150,000 a year had 337 and those earning more than $150,000 had just 172.

Interestingly, length of experience did not correlate with degree of success. Instead, "it's very much about getting focused and serving the right clients well," Bowen says.

"Fewer clients allow you the time you need to provide a consistent, high-quality experience, resulting in both better client retention and referrals," he adds.

Begin reaching for the upper echelon of your profession by defining who, for you, counts as an ideal client. Then reexamine whether your marketing messages send the right signals to those who fit your profile. If not, adjust them.

Just don't slim down your client list so far that you'd become vulnerable if a few died or left you!

∂∾ ∽ઝ

Action Steps

✦ Honestly assess whether you devote enough time, energy and care to all your clients. If not, is there a category of customer that tends not to get optimal results? Consider whether that's a category you should therefore stop serving.

✦ If you had fewer clients, what extra value could you offer them? Take a clear-headed look at that extra value and ponder whether you think clients would be willing to pay a premium for your above-and-beyond quality and service.

Pigeonhole Yourself, Part I

When *Marketing Minute* subscriber Jim Smith began calling himself The Executive Happiness Coach in 2006, he narrowed his niche from anyone needing executive coaching or leadership development to those who already understand the connection between workplace success and happiness.

Previously, when he didn't make explicit his viewpoint about the emotional component of good leadership, he'd experience resistance from executives, or a program wouldn't resonate with the organization.

"Now my brand serves as a useful sorting mechanism," he says. "If someone's first reaction to hearing 'The Executive Happiness Coach' is 'Eeeooo, touchy-feely stuff,' then I know they're not a good match for me."

About 30 percent of all his new business comes from his web site, where it's clear he believes emotions influence the and 55 percent derives from his presentations which normally include the word "happiness" in the session title or description.

"My close rate jumped tremendously with my up-front branding," he adds. "My prices are higher now, too. I'm no longer a commodity, as I was when I billed myself just as Jim Smith, president of People, Inc."

On the Web

Read an article describing ten copywriting techniques for warning away unsuitable clients and inviting ideal ones:

www.yudkin.com/idealcustomers.htm

Pigeonhole Yourself, Part II

At BestTrainingPractices.com, a link called "7 Reasons Not to Hire Me" leads to a page with biting, backhanded wit. For example:

> I have to be honest with you–there are a lot of consultants out there who seem to be able to spend their client's money faster than I can. If you're in a position to just fling tons of money at your problems in the hope that something works, you may come to find my questions about priorities, about applying communication and training resources to get the best return on your investment, annoying.

Will Kenny, the company owner, explains, "Before I decide to do business with someone, I prowl around their site to get a feel for what they're like, not just what they sell. That page sets up a snapshot for that to happen in one go.

"The style part of a relationship is crucial to the success of consulting. When people find that page overly flippant and decide not to work with me, that saves me the trouble of working with them and having a client firing later."

Action Steps

+ In the spirit of fun, create your own list of reasons why the people you'd rather not do business with should not hire you. In a more serious mood, determine whether you can and should convey some of those points diplomatically.

+ Imagine having a little elf you could send out to introduce you ahead of time so people would have exactly the right expectations of you, without anyone knowing the advance briefing came from you. What would you like the elf to communicate? Now how can you get the elf's message across indirectly?

The Snowflake Principle

Can businesses that deliver similar services be unique, like the snowflakes proved to be one of a kind 100 years ago by Vermont farmer/photographer Wilson Bentley? Yes.

Years ago I served as the behind-the-scenes copywriter for a consultant who advised a very narrow niche: translation agencies. Sarah had once owned an agency and helped struggling owners reach her previous pinnacle of success.

Before giving me marching orders to write a promotional letter for a new client, Sarah would tell me what to emphasize. For several dozen agencies during the years I wrote for her, she always managed to hand me a new angle for each new client. Thus my letters easily made every agency sound different from competitors.

One agency was the "go to" place for Latin American translations. Another specialized in translating contracts and documents for litigation. For another, their guarantee was the distinguishing mark. For another, fastest service; another had per-word pricing instead of quote-based fees. And on and on.

Like Bentley, the pioneering photographer of snowflakes, Sarah revealed uniqueness through passionately close attention to detail.

Action Steps

✦ Either by cataloguing actual competitors or by imagining them, list at least seven different strengths that might be claimed by someone in your industry. Which of these do or could apply to your organization? Select one and make it a centerpiece of a marketing campaign.

✦ Using colorful pictures cut out of magazines, create two collages—one of your ideal customer and the other of your most unwanted customer. With a red marker, add a heart to the first collage and draw a thick diagonal "not" across the other one. Hang these on the wall to ponder whenever you are writing or designing ads for your organization.

Part 3
The Dynamics of Trust

Attract Business Via Your Reputation

Want to shorten the sales cycle for your professional services? Want pre-sold prospects who need fewer or no face-to-face meetings before hiring you? Create a reputation.

Recently a room full of consultants agreed that you had to meet with potential clients at least twice—better, three times—before winning the business. "Then how do you get business outside the area?" someone asked. Their consensus: Forget it.

Yet I've been hired by companies in Australia and elsewhere without even phone calls, much less a face-to-face. Like nearly all my most congenial clients, they weren't choosing candidates to compare with one another. They weren't shopping, weren't engaged in a systematic search. If hunting, they stopped when they found me. Or they hadn't thought of spending money on their problem until my reputation gave them the idea.

With a reputation, you get more inquiries like "Do you do...?" and fewer along the lines of "We're looking for a _____ who does..." With a reputation, pre-sale meetings drop to one or zero. Email or phone exchanges can suffice. Powerful stuff!

❧   ❧

On the Web

Skeptical, like those consultants, that it's possible to book client projects without a preliminary face-to-face? Building a reputation greatly aids the process of transforming a local business to a virtual one. My recorded teleseminar on creating a virtual practice normally costs $37, but receive it free by inserting the coupon code STRATEGY in the shopping cart when you place your order at:

www.yudkin.com/virtual.htm

Truth or Lies?

You'd certainly want a photographer to position and light you in such a way as to produce a portrait that seems appealing and attractive. Where's the line between showing yourself at your best and deceiving your market?

A woman who asked me to review her press release said in it that she'd gone from cleaning toilets to owning the largest janitorial service in Delaware. Casually in conversation with me, she mentioned that that wasn't true–her company wasn't anywhere close to the largest. I suggested she change her materials accordingly. She didn't.

Someone else requesting my advice provided, along with a book proposal, bios and blurbs from catalogs that claimed he'd already published "numerous" books. He even gave a book title that, like the rest of these "numerous" achievements, didn't exist. I said he'd be jeopardizing the whole proposal to include these exhibits. But I'm not sure he'll leave them out.

When I presented these examples to *Marketing Minute* subscribers, I asked whether these examples stank of lying or counted as acceptable exaggeration. Of more than 100 replies, every one condemned these marketing miscreants as beneath contempt.

On the Web

Read selected comments from *Marketing Minute* subscribers on why stretching the truth and lying won't wash in business:

www.yudkin.com/truth.htm

Nothing But the Truth

Lying is in the news again. Not long after historian Joseph Ellis, a professor at Mount Holyoke College, won the Pulitzer Prize, the *Boston Globe* revealed he was falsely claiming to students and others that he'd fought in Vietnam. The incontrovertible evidence cast a dark shadow across his hitherto respected career.

Most professionals never fully recover from public exposure as liars. Remember this when you feel tempted to embellish!

A couple of months ago, someone wrote this to a business discussion list: "We are grateful to be a popular site on the Internet." When I visited his site, it looked spanking new to me, and I ran it through a link checker to see who was linking to it: nobody. When I asked the guy nicely for an explanation, he replied that by "popular" he didn't necessarily mean getting a lot of traffic. It was just marketing talk.

Sorry! People assume you mean what you write and judge you accordingly.

Don't make up achievements, stretch the truth or claim results that aren't so.

❧ ❧

Action Steps

+ Imagine someone has threatened to report your company to the Federal Trade Commission, the Better Business Bureau or another regulatory entity for untrue statements, but you have two business days before the complaint gets filed. In that time frame, find and correct any statements in your marketing that might rub the authorities the wrong way.

+ Be honest with yourself, and identify the three marketing situations in which it would be hardest for you to tell the truth. (For example: when you've made someone's short list; when promoting a brand-new product; when you're angry about a competitor getting ahead by telling untruths.) Explain convincingly to yourself why it's best to be honest even there.

Seek Influencers

Suppose you have a budget for mailings and a number of slots for lunchtime schmoozing. Dollar for dollar, hour for hour, you get the greatest return from your expenditure of money, time and energy when you focus on individuals in a position to recommend you to many, many folks.

Years ago, I sent *Marketing Minute* postcards to several hundred heads of speakers bureaus. Several who subscribed not only picked up tips for their own business but also urged speakers they represent to subscribe or call me for consulting. Ditto for directors of Small Business Development Centers, who can recommend my web site, books and newsletter week in and week out. Ditto for media people.

For your target market, who routinely comes into contact with prime potential clients? Who doesn't do what your company does but has the confidence of those who suffer from the problems you solve?

For a nanny agency, think about pediatricians.

For a same-day tailor, approach hotel concierges.

For a turnaround expert, meet with accountants.

Aim at people who represent a hub of influence!

Action Steps

+ Invite a potential influencer whom you already know out to lunch. Quiz him or her on the best ways for you to gain the attention of his or her colleagues and pitch them successfully on your advantages as a vendor or service provider.

+ List 10 influencers whose praise and recommendations of you would make it easier for you to sell to a certain group of customers. Create and execute a six-month plan for contacting those influencers repeatedly so they gradually know who you are and why customers should choose you to do business with.

Target Trendsetters

The #1 marketing move if you've invented some nifty high-tech gadget is sending samples to media people. If they use it and like it, they write about it or discuss it on the air. Word of mouth from those working for newspapers, magazines, radio and TV usually has an exponentially greater effect than excitement on the part of the kid down the block or the worker in the next cubicle.

In many cases, though, you should cultivate opinion leaders other than the media. Here's how Boston's Steve Adelman lures thousands to party in his six nightclubs. Promoters approach attractive young shoppers in fashionable stores and put them on the special reduced-price guest list for that night.

"There's a core group in this town of 200 or 300 people who others want to follow. When they're happy, the word spreads," says Adelman.

hen 3M introduced Post-it Notes, it sent
taries, who evangelized for the yellow sticky
notes throughout the office, at their churches and at home.
Have you targeted the trendsetters in your industry?

Action Steps

+ Analyze the characteristics of potential customers
  who are especially open to what's new and who love
  to tell their peers what they've discovered. Like Steve
  Adelman in the story above, figure out where you can
  most easily run across them. Based on your analysis,
  come up with a plan for approaching trendsetters and
  getting them to try your stuff.

+ With your marketing team, brainstorm characteristics that might prove to be a royal turnoff to trendsetters, then figure out how to avoid all the turnoffs
  when you approach your opinion shapers.

+ Craft a special offer that would leave the average person cold but might be irresistible to a trendsetter.

Indirectly Break Through the Pack

Try an indirect approach to gain entry to an opportunity where there's a glut of supplicants.

Writer Lawrence Grobel used this strategy when he wanted to do celebrity interviews for *Playboy* magazine. Instead of sending editorial queries and thus joining a pack of wannabees, he interviewed *Playboy* mogul Hugh Hefner for *Newsday* and did an especially thorough job. Hefner then passed Grobel along to the proper editor at *Playboy*, for whom he interviewed Barbra Streisand, Marlon Brando and others. Mission accomplished!

I took the roundabout route too when I identified desirable blurb writers for the first edition of my book *6 Steps to Free Publicity.* Since a request for a blurb can feel like an imposition from a stranger, I introduced myself earlier by interviewing them, including their stories in the book and later asking for and getting their endorsement.

when I decided to pursue representation by speakers' bureaus, I knew they receive dozens of inquiries from speakers every week. Instead of joining those wannabees, I sent postcards detailing how I could help them in their marketing. One bureau hired me, then booked me—precisely as hoped!

Action Steps

+ Invite three friends or colleagues to lunch and share stories about how you each managed to meet and impress hard-to-know people. Implement at least one of the strategies that worked for a lunchmate.

+ "Show, don't tell": Use this well-known maxim of writing teachers as a guideline by figuring out how you can demonstrate the qualities you want to be known for, instead of just saying you have those qualities. Then decide how you can get your demonstration in front of the people whose attention you want.

Non-Disclosure Agreements: Caution

If I had a nickel for every entrepreneur who's walked into my office and asked me to sign a non-disclosure agreement, I could chuck it all and move to Tahiti. Every time this happens, I see a huge red flag pop out of the top of their head: Warning! Careful!"

So says Rob Adams, who invests in high-tech ventures through his company in Austin, Texas, AV Labs. Protection has its place, he concedes. But this behavior tends to go with grossly unrealistic visions of the commercial potential of a pet idea and failure to understand how much hard work and savvy implementation contribute to success.

Just yesterday someone who had already half-sold me on participating in an Internet project lost me when they suddenly jammed a hitherto unmentioned non-disclosure and non-compete agreement into the process. Who in the world would agree not to compete for a year with an idea that hadn't even been revealed yet? I might already have had this idea on my own.

Be prudent, but be reasonable in seeking marketing partners.

Action Steps

+ Before taking any step motivated by fear of someone ripping you off, consult with veterans of your industry—those with 20 or more years of experience—and listen to whether they believe your fears are reasonable or overblown.

+ Apart from signed documents, what are three indicators of trustworthiness that have proved reliable for you in the past? Outline a program for observing and investigating these indicators before revealing key details to potential partners.

Hold Certain Things Close to Your Chest

In one class, no one showed up after the first session, but no one asked for a refund, either. We made $45,000 with just about no work."

The above appeared in a case study about a management education company that ran high-priced seminars with low participation from enrollees. This quote bothered me, so much that it lingered in my mind for months.

Anyone who sells information products or consulting has had the experience of clients never cracking open the books they bought or not implementing advice for which they paid dearly. Students and clients can lack commitment and follow-through, and they often accept responsibility for that, rather than demand a refund. But bragging about that doesn't come off well. It verges on boasting that one has found a way to part people from their money without giving them anything in return.

When you're interviewed about your successes, remember that people always view what you say through the lens of their values, not yours. Some truths about your business are better kept to yourself.

Action Step

+ List ten things you've had reason to be happy about lately regarding your business. One by one, go back through the list and consider whether someone who didn't know you could take that point of pride as something to criticize. Whenever the answer is "yes," ask yourself whether, on balance, you should crow about that success or keep it to yourself.

Confidential Clients? Here's What to Do

S uppose you perform work that many clients prefer to keep confidential, such as plastic surgery, embezzlement investigations or marital counseling. People thinking about hiring you would like evidence of your excellence at what you do. Yet happy customers would die rather than let you quote their spontaneous, eloquent delight at the results you helped them achieve.

One solution to the secrecy: case studies.

In a case study, describe the initial problem as occurring not to your client but to someone in a general category that he, she or it falls into: "A senior manager in the manufacturing sector...," "A TV broadcaster who developed adult-onset acne...," "A branch office of a Big Five brokerage firm..."

After describing the individual's or organization's problem, present the solution or remedy you devised.

The final ingredient of a case study clinches its usefulness for marketing purposes. Make sure you include the benefits or results arising from your solution. "The TV station not only renewed its contract with the broadcaster, but another offer came in from a national network." "The firm passed the audit with flying colors."

Action Steps

✦ To choose suitable subjects for case studies, look over a list of clients for the last three years and select those who had an initial challenge others can identify with and who experienced a dramatic resolution of the challenge.

✦ Before making public any case study based on confidential circumstances, put your version of the situation aside for at least a few days. Then carefully look through what you've written, pondering whether you've included any telltale details that would clue people in on the individual or company you're discussing. The ultimate test of whether you've disguised cases enough is when clients don't realize they're the ones you've written about!

Reflections on Refunds

John Carlton writes: "A good marketer should be getting around 7-15 percent refunds." According to this way of thinking, if hardly anyone is requesting refunds, you're "not selling hard enough."

Although I understand the mathematical rationale for this concept, I couldn't tolerate even a 2 percent rate without a brain transplant. To me, a 7 percent rate would be an abomination.

The thought of that many people who were unhappy with what they ordered, who expected something other than what they got, appalls me. How could it be a good thing to deliberately generate negative energy? Remember that for every refund request, others were equally unhappy but did not ask for their money back.

And what kind of person doesn't care about the letdowns and disillusionment they are causing?

For me, successful marketing attracts exactly the people who want what I have to sell, persuades them to take the leap to buy and turns away those who represent a mismatch.

If I'm leaving revenue on the table, so be it. My goal is to generate happy customers–and an honorable reputation.

On the Web

I asked *Marketing Minute* subscribers for their opinion on this issue, and received nearly 100 thoughtful comments. Read them at:

www.yudkin.com/refunds.htm

You'd Better Learn About the Law

I was startled to learn that in my state, gift certificates have to be redeemable for at least two years, and must be turned into the state abandoned-property office if unredeemed after three years. The long arm of the law governs many aspects of marketing, and it pays to be informed.

I once met an astrologer who couldn't advertise in the local paper or post an outdoor sign because her Massachusetts town still had an eighteenth-century law on the books against "fortune tellers."

In the United States, federal laws cover ways in which you can promote a product that doesn't yet exist, when you can use the phrase "Going out of business," whether you can qualify a guarantee or a claim with an asterisk and much more.

How can you avoid violating laws that the average person hasn't heard of? First, join a professional association–most monitor laws affecting members. Second, consult governmental business law sites, such as the Federal Trade Commission's http://www.ftc.gov/bcp/guides/guides.htm (for the US). Third, contact a business attorney for a checkup.

Ignorance doesn't shield you from a crackdown!

Action Steps

+ If you've never given any thought to regulations that may apply to you in your country, state or locality, make an appointment with a business development counselor or an attorney knowledgeable about your industry, as a good starting point.

+ If you believe you've already covered most of your legal bases, find and subscribe to a publication that is very likely to inform you when new regulations come down the pike.

Part 4
Strategic Sales Boosters

Follow Up for a Competitive Edge

Some years back, professional speaker Patricia Fripp received a letter from someone who said he was writing to her and 19 other people whose profiles he'd selected from the National Speakers Association directory. "We'd like to hire you to give three speeches in the Cayman Islands and Palm Springs, and also pay you to attend an industry event. Please send information."

Fripp later learned that of the 20 people, she was the only one who sent the information fast, sent everything needed to make a decision, followed up to make sure he'd received everything and did not apologize for something.

Another time she responded to an email from a man looking through speakers' web sites and learned that of 60 people he'd emailed, only she and five others had responded.

"All I ever wanted in business was an unfair advantage," Fripp says. Unbelievably, what should be common sense of promptly following up on leads and acting professionally is uncommon even among top-ranking professionals. Doing the right things right gives you an edge over everyone else.

Action Steps

+ Rate yourself honestly on how often you respond to requests for information quickly and completely. If it's less than 75 percent of the time, think of steps you can take to improve your reply rate.

+ Rate yourself on how often you follow up at least once after providing information to a potential client who requested it. If it's less than 75 percent of the time, consider what you can do to increase your follow-up rate.

Simplify Decision Making

I'm not sure how to get started."

In a *Marketing Minute* poll about difficult client situations, many respondents mentioned clients who didn't know what they needed or wanted, or who took up too much uncompensated time figuring that out. Here's help for that dilemma.

First, ask enough questions to get a sense of the scope of the problem and the potential client's resources. If it's a $10,000 sort of need from an organization in a position to solve it, it's certainly worth spending 30 minutes in probing discussion.

Then tell the client clearly and with confidence what you recommend as a first step. First-time clients often prefer getting started with a chunk of the whole project that provides a low-risk taste of what it's like to work with you. Likewise, if you sell products, don't automatically recommend the super-deluxe (super-expensive) package to a new customer.

According to studies summarized by Doug Hall in *Meaningful Marketing,* reducing the number of options boosts sales.

In addition, create compelling special offers that give strangers a specific way to get started as your client.

Action Steps

✦ Think back to the last few times someone approached your firm without a clear sense of what they wanted or needed. Did you deal with that prospect effectively? If not, create two alternate scenarios in which you help the potential client focus on a project plan or first step. Decide how to handle this situation differently next time.

✦ Create at least one starter plan that gives new clients a way to experience doing business with you and then to continue with greater confidence.

Cross-Selling for Success

"Would you like fries with that?" Marketers call such a question "cross-selling," and it's as applicable to legal services and other high-priced offerings as to fast food. Without prompting, clients don't normally think about what other needs of theirs you might satisfy. Unless you make certain everyone who does business with you knows all the services and products you provide, some will walk across the street for stuff they could buy from you.

If you regard cross-selling as a program you might implement someday when you get around to it, consider this study reported in *Up the Loyalty Ladder* by Murray and Neil Raphel. When a customer had a checking account with a bank, the bank had a 50 percent chance of keeping that customer. If the customer had a checking and savings account there, those odds soared to 91 percent. When customers also had a loan with the bank, retention probability went up to 95 percent. Adding in a safe deposit box, it rose to 99 percent.

Cross-selling helps retain clients—and is profitable, too.

Action Steps

+ For one week, keep track of every time a company (or an individual) tries to cross-sell you, and rate each attempt as persuasive or not. What lessons can you draw from your observations for your own selling?

+ Think of at least five situations where you missed the opportunity to cross-sell. For each situation, ponder how your neglect of cross-selling shortchanged both the customer and you. Take notes on what you'll do differently to prevent such lost opportunities in the future.

From One-timers to Long-timers

How can I get customers to order again?" asks a *Marketing Minute* subscriber. "Too many order from me once and I never see them again."

Perfectly satisfied customers switch to Vendor B because they couldn't remember Vendor A or they perceived no difference between A and B.

Minimize one-timers with one or more of these strategies:

+ Discuss the big picture with them before delivering your goods or services. What are their goals and how can you help beyond their immediate need?

+ Provide "what's next" tips or promotions with their purchase. Plant ideas of what else they can accomplish with your assistance.

+ Create a rewards program, with a free widget after X orders.

- ✦ Establish an online membership program (free or paid) in which members exchange ideas and you answer questions in the realm of your expertise.
- ✦ Send autoresponder emails after a first purchase, containing suggestions, success stories and promotions.
- ✦ Send the same kind of content on postcards—some people pay more attention to these than to emails.

Don't let them forget you, and make the business relationship obviously worth their while!

Action Steps

- ✦ Create a chart with a list of your products or services in the left-hand column. Beside each item, write down what you can do before, during and after customers buy it to encourage repeat purchases.
- ✦ If you're not getting repeat customers, look closely at the marketing copy you're using, and figure out at least three ways to change it so it implies that repeat business is a normal occurrence at your company.

Attract or Chase?

In the January 2007 issue of *Inc.* magazine, a fascinating piece chronicles the saga of a top-drawer branding company that chased after a company owner who hadn't been thinking of a brand overhaul.

Intrigued by a series of witty hostage notes, Dave Hirschkop, creator of Insanity Sauce, 36 times hotter than Tabasco, agreed to the offer of a complimentary brand makeover from Deskey, a branding firm.

The branders needed a fun creative project, and Hirschkop was open to the idea of revamping his 136-product line, grouped under the moniker of Dave's Gourmet.

Creative teams at Deskey then came up with five new brand options, along with a sixth approach the firm recommended. In personality, they ranged from edgy and irreverent to classy and refined.

Which rebranding did Hirschkop choose? None of them. Emotionally, he's still married to his Insanity theme and suspects his customers are, too.

To me, the story shows that a zillion creative light bulbs can't convince a company owner to change unless he first felt the need to do so.

The most effective marketing attracts. It does not chase.

Action Steps

+ Rate yourself on a scale of 1 to 10 according to how much you prefer to attract business (1) or chase it (10). If you scored above 7, try waiting to chase until after people express an interest in what you are selling, and see if that increases your success. If you scored below 3, try adding more follow-up to your marketing routine, and see if that improves results.

+ Formulate and test questions for potential clients that reveal their readiness to make the kind of changes in their business that are part and parcel of doing business with you.

Harness Attraction

Although in some quarters, the bestselling DVD and book *The Secret* are disparaged as mystical claptrap, I salute producer/author Rhonda Byrne for focusing attention on the idea that success in life begins with how you think and what you believe. You broadcast that to the universe, and the universe responds.

During my coaching of business owners over the years, I've seen innumerable instances of the principle that we get what we ask for. When someone feels frustrated because the "wrong" customers are showing up, there's often something I can help pinpoint in his or her beliefs, attitudes, wording or behavior that has invited those supposedly unwelcome responders.

Change the signals being sent out, and the response changes, too.

In marketing, the dynamic can be subtle and challenging because we often don't realize childhood experiences are ur expectations and what others pick up from us. Prospective clients bolt when they sense doubt, phoniness or desperation. On the other hand, when they perceive a match between their needs and what comes across from you, they sign on.

With self-awareness, attraction marketing works in your favor.

❧　❦

Action Steps

+ Ask a mentor, coach, mastermind group or trusted colleague what signals they notice you putting out that might affect the kinds of customers who show up.

+ If you're unhappy with the results you're getting in your business, ask yourself, "What am I doing to attract this situation?" Let the question percolate in your mind, and be willing to consider the answers that rise up from your intuition.

+ When the results you want aren't showing up, ask yourself, "What's the hidden payoff in not getting what I want?" Again, give a fair hearing to the possible answers that emerge.

A Customer Question is a Gift

Not sure which product or service to develop next? For insights into urgent needs, simply watch your email.

Technical consultant Melanie Mendelson of Chicago found gold when someone asked her advice on dealing with a programmer who wasn't completing a project the way she wanted it.

"I realized I'd met a lot of other business owners who'd gotten burned by tech people—and with my background in programming, I had insider knowledge on the topic," she says. The result: Mendelson's ebook, *Profitable Outsourcing.*

For David Badurina, questions from actual and potential customers shaped the refinement of his software application, Viral Marketing Tool—how the program prints, how it inter-acts with web sites, how he tracks statistics for it and more.

For me, customer questions have driven updates. "I'm looking at buying your report, but it says 'Revised for 2008.' Are you planning a 2009 revision?" I had my assistant drop

:ck all the links, changing everything that

, I had a 2009 edition.

or from-left-field questions can provide

valuable market clues!

⤸ ⤷

Action Steps

✦ Create a system for collecting questions that are coming in from actual and potential clients and a time-
line for reviewing them at least several times a year.
Consider especially whether they point to strategic
opportunities you can easily pursue.

✦ Think of five changes you can implement to encourage more customer questions, and implement at least
two of them.

Fending Off Free Advice Seekers

In a *Marketing Minute* survey on troublesome client relationships, about 45 percent of respondents said they were bedeviled by clients who kept asking for free advice.

You can head off a good portion of that from paying clients by setting down in writing what your fees cover and do not cover. While you don't want to come off as some sort of dictator with a stringent rulebook, it helps to set forth guidelines for a productive relationship.

Some copywriters, for instance, clearly specify conditions like these:

+ the number of revisions included in a quoted fee
+ the number of days within which clients must request those revisions
+ average time from order to completion
+ supplying all research is the client's responsibility

For inquiries from folks who are not yet clients, feel free to copy what I do. If I can answer a question in five minutes or less, I generally just go ahead and do so. If a question is more complicated than that, I reply, "I couldn't do justice to your question without a consultation. My consulting rates are..."

Prevent hassles by making expectations explicit!

On the Web

If you feel that people are always trying to pick your brains without paying or you're troubled by the idea of giving away free information, listen to a coaching session in which I help a consultant through such fears. It's a downloadable audio, free just for readers of this book:

www.yudkin.com/freeseekers.htm

Cooperate With Competitors

Before I moved to the country, I was taken aback to spot a brand-new FedEx drop-off box at the foot of the stairs to my local post office. As I waited in line to send packages, though, I reflected that it made a lot of sense for these two organizations that you'd think would be competitors to intertwine with each other.

Both deliver packages. FedEx is more expensive and reliable. The US Postal Service delivers on weekends for no extra charge, and handles letters as well. Where I used to live, many FedEx drop-off boxes had hard-to-find addresses in office parks, while practically everywhere, locals know the post office.

In short, it benefits both enterprises to have the other on the spot. FedEx gets an easy-to-find, convenient location while the Postal Service probably picks up business from folks who intended to use FedEx but decided to use the cheaper option.

Ponder this before you repeat today's platitudes that business is war, competitors are to-the-death enemies and you must annihilate your customers' other options to survive!

Action Steps

+ Identify three to five direct competitors. Think of the most compelling reasons to cooperate, and make overtures accordingly.

+ Identify three to five indirect competitors, where your offerings overlap slightly. Again ponder the strongest reasons to join forces, and pursue the connections that make the most sense.

Tying in With a Cause

B reast cancer is the best thing that ever happened to me."
One doesn't expect to encounter such a statement upon arriving at a web site selling nutritious treats. Yet that's the lead for the site of Goodness Gracious, Inc., offering all-natural cookies "free of cancer-causing additives and chemicals."

I can't recall ever seeing a more appealing instance of blending do-good motivations with solid business sense. Company founder Grace Geniusz, a former nurse, produced more than 1.2 million cookies in 2000 and donates 10 percent of after-tax profits to breast cancer research. Her mission is to wake people up to the danger of food additives and to promote the sorts of research that saved her life.

By citing venues that serve her cookies, like Alaska Airlines, the site bolsters her credibility. With details of her fundraising efforts, Geniusz's sincerity becomes impossible to doubt.

Breast cancer research, laptops for the poor, literacy initiatives, animal rescue, microloans for women in poverty-stricken countries–these are uncontroversial causes. Make sure yours is, also.

❧ ☙

On the Web

Got a feel-good mission statement? Don't expect the way you've worded it for yourself to be a motivational marketing message for others. Read more about the reasons for keeping mission statements in-house, and comments from dozens of *Marketing Minute* subscribers, at:

www.yudkin.com/missions.htm

Business is local

* Heifer Int'l

* KIVA.org

* Microloans

who's the Indian who doesn't believe in profit?

The Best Giveaways

Y ours free!" It's a rare head that doesn't turn at that news. Offer freebies keyed to the interests and desires of your target market and take advantage of this powerful psychological appeal to grow your business.

Great giveaway strategy begins with a wisely chosen free item. You'll be tempted to give away something you sell as a promotion, but according to online publicity specialist Steve O'Keefe, this is a mistake, undercutting the perceived value of the giveaway product.

Instead, the best giveaway is something people can get only through your special offer. They can't buy it from you and they can't get it from another supplier, either.

Giveaways work especially well as a bonus for a certain number or dollar value of sales. The Talisman Billiards Accessories Company in Thailand offers a free golf shirt for every offer over $70. "A lot of people increase their order to get the free bonus," says *Marketing Minute* subscriber Tony Jones, Talisman's general manager.

According to veteran marketer Rene Gnam, giveaway incentives can increase sales as much as 40 percent. Customers win, and you do too.

Action Steps

✦ Think about what you have or can obtain that's unique and desirable to your target market or a segment of it, perhaps involving exclusivity, access, a privilege, recognition or scarcity. Then build a promotion around that freebie, offering it to the first X buyers, or anyone spending more than $Y prior to a certain date.

✦ Find a complementary business and team up for giveaways where you offer the other company's item with a purchase from you and they do likewise for you with their customers.

Dancing the Old Two-Step

Several public radio stations run thematic tours to inter-esting places, enabling listeners to learn about Berlin's musical heritage or the ecosystem of Barbados. They can't sell you on a $3,000 tour in a 30-second or even 60-second spot. Instead, they invite you to a free lecture. Or they tempt you to visit the tour description on the station's site.

When you're marketing something complicated or ex-pensive, proceeding in two steps works best.

In Step 1, coax interested parties to learn more. Provide just enough detail to whet their appetite, aligning everything in your marketing pitch to motivate a certain response, such as attending a meeting, placing a call, sending back a request form or going to a web page.

In Step 2, provide all the information prospects need to make their buying decision—and follow up, follow up, follow up.

Don't muck up the process by making it possible for people to buy from Step 1. They're not ready at that point. It's also too early to load them up with facts, reasons, benefits or incentives.

Orchestrate your marketing to hear the cash register sing!

Action Steps

+ Remember times when you have attempted to sell people on an expensive product or service right off the bat. Redesign the sales process so you sell people first on an intermediary step that winnows the interested from the not-interested.

+ If you have already implemented two-step marketing, look for ways to improve your follow-up by email, telephone or mail.

The Two-Step Fills Your Dance Card

To sell high-priced products and services, use a two-step process. In Step 1, put forth something of high value that provides a free or low-cost chance to experience what you have to offer. In Step 2, follow up with those who came forward and expressed interest.

Proven options for Step 1:

+ Printed information sent on request. Tangible items may stick around desks and files for ages, pulled out again when a need becomes acute.
+ Online information. Sending people to an intriguing article on your web site tempts many to poke around while there, discovering more about your firm.
+ Needs analysis. A no-cost, no-obligation evaluation of a potential client's needs gets you up close and personal so you can present a high-data, low-pressure reason to buy.

✦ Event. Prospects who attend your lecture, networking party or demonstration step into your world, experiencing a face-to-face appreciation of your style, expertise and personality.

✦ Trial. Whether no-cost or low-cost, a limited-time trial can get perfect prospects hooked on your product or service, happily continuing as a customer.

On the Web

When you've settled on a tantalizing item for Step 1 in two-step marketing, publicize it with a press release. The following page includes a sample press release for a "bait piece" whose format you can model:

www.yudkin.com/bait.htm

Strategically Structure Options

Several moviemakers have created humor through a scene where a patron in a restaurant laboriously orders something not on the menu. This reveals the patron's character and helps advance the plot because most restaurant goers select from the options they're presented with.

Because of this quirk of human behavior, the options you present in your marketing materials and in proposals have an enormous influence on what people order, even when you also accommodate many off-menu requests.

Most buyers are compliant, notes Alan Weiss in his book *Value-Based Fees: How to Charge–and Get–What You're Worth.* By providing three options, you move prospects from pondering whether or not to hire you to pondering which option to choose.

"Over the course of my entire career, buyers have chosen my least expensive option less than 10 percent of the time, and my most expensive option over 35 percent of the time," Weiss says.

By adding more and even more value to the deluxe and super-deluxe options, you coax buyers to spend more, a dynamic that doesn't occur with one "take it or leave it" choice.

Action Steps

✦ Where you have only one option, add deluxe and super-deluxe options, with added items, more customization, higher quality ingredients or faster service.

✦ If you already have three tiered options, with a majority of customers choosing the most expensive package, create an ultra-ultra option that's even more pricey than that, and drop the least expensive package. Research shows the new tiers should increase profits.

Be There at the Right Time

Last week, I registered my affiliate program in online directories. Just as I wanted to scream from the tedium of the process, I received an email from a directory I'd contacted offering to register my program with 40 directories for a small fee. Talk about a timely offer!

It reminded me of a billboard in front of an apartment complex near downtown Boston, facing rush-hour drivers: "If you lived here, you'd be home now."

Can you likewise show up when or where prospective buyers are feeling maximum frustration?

+ Is there a season when those you sell to may feel down or discouraged? If your service typically lowers someone's tax bill, get a message into the mail the month income tax returns are due.

+ Is there some location where you can reach people when they fervently wish for the results you provide?

Dressing-room mirrors, for instance, for weight-loss programs.

+ Is there a product or service folks buy that signals they badly need you? Perhaps new members of a gym are psychologically ready for therapy, too.

Timeliness is profitable.

Action Steps

+ List at least four seasonal events when people are (or could be) psychologically primed to buy what you sell. If seasonal promotions are already epidemic in your industry, find offbeat holidays to link to in *Chase's Calendar of Events,* available at most public libraries.

+ Survey your customer base to learn what internal or external events may have prompted them to decide the time was right for them to buy.

Strategic Surveys Get You Noticed

Trying to gain entrée to top decision makers? Try this.

1. Choose one survey question to which your target market would love to know the answer.

2. Ask top decision makers to reply to the survey question, promising they'll get the tabulated results before you make them public.

3. Send the top decision makers (even those who didn't respond to the survey) a report of the survey results, concluding with a soft-sell profile of your firm.

4. Follow up with an offer to the decision makers for a free one-on-one executive briefing on the topic of the survey.

5. Distribute a press release to the target industry on your survey findings.

6. When an article about the survey gets published, send a copy to each decision maker with whom you didn't yet get a meeting. Attach a handwritten stick-on note saying "I

thought you'd be interested in this." Then call these decision makers again.

When your survey reveals something of value to your target market, you begin establishing a reputation—or solidifying one already started—with this group.

On the Web

I've provided additional suggestions on creating newsworthy research at:

www.yudkin.com/newsworthy.htm

Become an Octopus

Are you overly reliant on just one or two ways people can discover what you sell?

Nick Usborne sent me his new book, *New Path to Riches*, which explains how to earn extra income online by becoming "the expert next door."

Nick designed this $19.95 paperback so it both stands on its own and also funnels readers to his $397 home-study course if they'd like more depth.

"I wrote the book to reach tens of thousands of non-Internet-obsessed people that I'm not reaching now," he told me. "Some book readers will buy the course to learn step by step how to build a money-making website."

It took Nick 15 days to outline it, 30 days to write it and 30 days to set it up for publication with a print-on-demand company.

Just as people looking for books may not be doing general searches online, some folks avidly watch videos, listen to podcasts or depend on radio or their librarian to recommend what's worth their attention.

Become an octopus, with arms outstretched to multiple realms where people can discover you.

Action Steps

+ Get together with four or five non-competing business owners, and share information about kinds of outreach you each do and all the ways customers find your respective companies. Before the end of this meeting, identify at least two more octopus arms you're going to add to your marketing plan.

+ Create a list of all the octopus arms you've ever had going for your business. Identify at least two methods of outreach that seem to have worked well but that you haven't used lately, then decide how to redeploy them.

The Bigfoot Strategy

In some niches, unsophisticated customers search in droves for something that you, the professional, know doesn't work.

Instead of feeling frustrated and angry that charlatans are snatching much of the business, use what I call the Bigfoot Strategy, named after the legendary ape-like creature whose sightings scientists have not been able to squelch.

Identify a phrase that the naive ones search for. Then use it prominently and honestly in the title of an article or the headline of a press release that explains the shortcomings of the mythical entity they're looking for.

For example:

Fix Your Own Wiring? Five Reasons Why It's Safer to Call a Licensed Electrician

Free Online Translation Sites: A Quick Way to Become a Laughingstock–and An Affordable Alternative

Why You Can't Become a Black Belt in a Weekend, and Other Secrets From a Young World-Class Martial Artist

Hire a Cheap, Fast Ad Agency and Repent in Leisure, Says Albuquerque Marketing Consultant

With this strategy, you attract attention, stand out amidst the competition, educate potential customers and win enough of them over to make the effort worthwhile.

Action Step

+ List the ridiculous myths, unscrupulous come-ons and naive hopes in your industry. Determine the exact phraseology used in these instances of wishful thinking. Then craft a headline or article title both using that precise language and debunking it. Follow through by writing the rest of the piece and distributing it.

Part 5
Stay in Touch, Stay in Touch

Repetition is Required

Many people believe that when someone you contact does not buy, you have failed. In fact, you're just getting started.

A few months ago I sat with a prospective client who had requested a meeting. When he opened a file, I could scarcely believe what I saw: close to a dozen of my marketing pieces, going back to December 1992. Some of them I myself no longer had copies of.

"You've been keeping track of me for that long?" I asked, in shock.

"Uh-huh."

"I'm curious—how many times do you think you heard from me or about me before you picked up the phone to call me?"

"Mmm, probably seventeen."

Seventeen times! This story comes closer to the rule than to the exception. Repetition is crucial in marketing.

The first couple of times someone hears from or about you barely make a dent in a prospect's memory. After six or seven times, there's recognition, but perhaps not a current need just yet.

Whether the requisite number of contacts is seven or seventeen, make repetition a cornerstone of your marketing plan.

≈ ∾

Action Steps

✦ Taking into account your own personality and the likely communication preferences of your target market, decide on your optimal media for follow-up: mail, email, telephone or repeat lunch engagements. Formulate a realistic plan specifying the frequency of repeated contact in those media.

✦ Ask new customers how long they'd had their eye on you before they made their first purchase, and prepare to be surprised.

Why Persistence Pays

How many times should you follow up when someone seems sincerely interested but doesn't sign on the bottom line? Most of us give up too soon, say sales experts. Recently I experienced this with a web site I fully intend to do business with.

After I registered to list my seminars and products at a training supersite, a representative offered me a free 60-day trial of a related service. This offer required me to fill out very detailed forms, and I couldn't find the time to do so. The rep called four or five times to ask if I had any questions, and each time we connected I told him I was indeed interested.

When I still did not submit my form, the rep must have concluded that I wasn't serious. I was and am serious. But this is something I'd rather take care of in August, not in June.

Are you too quick to assume that someone who doesn't sign on soon won't ever do so? Sometimes, as with me, your eager time line does not jibe with the prospect's priorities. Keep following up instead of assuming interest has died.

Action Steps

+ Reflect on the number of times you typically contact someone who had expressed interest before giving up with the assumption that they are no longer interested. Commit yourself to increasing that average by trying them a couple of times more.

+ Develop a spiel that can put you in a positive mindset for persistently following up with prospects. Write it down or find an image or posture that reminds you of the virtue of politely keeping the connection going.

Repeat Those Customer Contacts!

Troubled by the number of people who inquire about your products or services and then disappear? You should be. Within a year, around 80% of those who make such inquiries end up buying what they asked about—not necessarily from the company they originally contacted.

A series of sales letters or emails—three or more sent one to two weeks apart—can help ensure that you snag the sale that might go to your competitor. Follow-up calls perform the same function. The first contact motivates the prospect, but not enough. The second pushes him or her closer to action, and it may take the third or fourth or seventh or eighth contact to make the prospect feel the readiness and urgency to act.

When you do come up with a sequence and frequency of messages that gets results, repeating it to the very same group will bring you half again of the original response, experts say.

Don't worry that repeated contact will turn off those who were interested. It's far more likely that a potential buyer who becomes ready to buy has forgotten you because you didn't appear often enough.

Action Steps

✦ If you don't already have one, create a comprehensive system of follow-up, from the first tentative email or phone call to the first sale and beyond. Set it up so the system is either completely automated or turned into a company routine.

✦ If you have a system of follow-up that is working well, add a few additional contacts to the system. If those work well, too, add a few more, until the point at which results level off.

Why Stay in Touch, Part I

The other day I thought about a couple whose workshops I had taken and whose books I'd bought and studied about six years ago. Where are they now? What new perspectives have they developed that I've missed?

In the last six years, I've received two or three mailings from them, and none in the last three years. Have they retired? Died? I suspect they've just let me slip out of their sphere of influence. Alas!

As marketers we usually look at staying in touch with customers as a means to fully exploit opportunities to sell. Rarely do we think about what continued contact means for the customer. It's an opportunity to revisit the needs satisfied in previous sales encounters, the chance to enrich their lives through the purchase of related products and services.

When you fail to keep in touch with customers, you make it harder for them to scratch whatever itch led them to do business with you. Don't be so cruel. Stay in touch with past buyers at least three times a year—for their sake, if not for yours.

Action Steps

+ List at least four ways in which your continuing to stay in touch with customers benefits them. Then plan marketing campaigns to your customer base that bring those reasons to stay in touch to the forefront, especially for those who may not have bought in a while.

+ Calculate the average length of time that customers stay with you, and resolve to increase that average next year. Identify specific steps you've read about in this book to include in your marketing plan to make that happen.

Why Stay in Touch, Part II

D o you stay in touch with clients you've finished working for? I read this story on a discussion list.

Emily O'Connor of Pine Bush, NY, used three consultants to refine and upgrade the web site she'd created. Although all did their best to help her at the time, not one contacted her later to see how she was doing. Nor did they visit her web site–www.photo-gift-centers.com–afterwards to see how it was progressing.

"As a retired direct marketing consultant," O'Connor wrote, "I find this inconceivable. One of my commandments in my business was to contact every client at least once a year to keep up with their progress. Many times this brought more business, but most often, it showed my concern for how my past suggestions had helped them, and for how much benefit they had received from my consultation. It was so appreciated that it led to hundreds of referrals for new business."

Hundreds of referrals! Are you willing to invest the energy to contact each past client of yours once per year and reap that kind of harvest?

Action Steps

✦ Develop a brief, friendly questionnaire you can send to clients on the first, third and fifth year anniversaries of completing a major project with them. Like Emily O'Connor, ask how that project was continuing to work for them. When completed questionnaires come back, send a personal thank-you for each one.

✦ Team up with three non-competing companies that serve the same market. Pool your mailing lists of paying customers, and send a small, useful gift every quarter from one of the participating partners.

Make New Customers, Keep the Old

Every time I've led a seminar for bankers, someone has asked, "How can we prevent current customers from taking advantage of incentives for new customers?"

Banks are not alone in this predicament.

In testing done by Jakob Nielsen, users tend to "complain bitterly" when an online checkout procedure includes an option for entering a discount code and they don't have one. Who wants to pay more for an item than other customers?

Ways to attract new customers without alienating existing ones include:

✦ Offer discriminatory bonuses or discounts only when you can control who sees these offers, such as through direct mail, not in newspaper ads

✦ Send new customers to a just-for-them web page with separate shopping cart options

✦ Choose bonuses you can afford to give everyone

If an existing customer does learn about a promotion to new customers and asks for the same deal, simply give it to them without argument.

By the way, research shows it's five times easier and more profitable to sell to current customers than to lure new ones. Make sure you have your marketing priorities straight!

Action Steps

+ Every time you develop an initiative to attract new customers, balance it with something special you're doing to retain existing ones.

+ Calculate your churn rate–the ratio of the number of customers who stop doing business with you over your total number of active customers. Resolve to improve the churn rate next year. Identify specific steps you've read about in this book to include in your marketing plan to make that happen.

Only Reconnect

Years ago, Bob Bly wrote an article on marketing your way through a recession. He suggested that simply by calling past clients to say hello and to find out what was going on in their business, you would get an average of one out of ten giving you a new assignment simply because you showed up in their awareness at an opportune time.

My experience bears this out. A new client, an attorney, asked me what kind of work I'd previously done for attorneys. So I contacted two lawyer clients to find out whether or not I could give their names as references to the new client.

Two out of two, in addition to saying "of course," asked if I could help them out with a current project.

"Warning: Don't call up and say, 'I'm not busy and need work right now; do you have any assignments?'" says Bly.

In one case, before sending my email, I visited the past client's web site and learned he had won a major publishing award. Congratulating him on that news was a perfect way to reestablish our connection.

Action Steps

✦ Develop a list of at least five good reasons to get in touch with clients you're not currently working with. Pull this out whenever business gets slow. Use a notebook or a computerized contact manager to keep track of those you get back in touch with, when and with what result.

✦ Do the same for referral sources–those who have sent you customers in the past.

Reactivating Customers

An imaginative magazine ad from the McCormick spice company shows a spice bottle label with two lines circled. "If you see 'Baltimore, MD' on the label, the spice is at least 15 years old." The ad also shows a red and white spice tin: "Except for black pepper, McCormick spices in rectangular tins are at least 15 years old."

They didn't need to add that these ultra-old spices should be replaced. That message comes through loud and clear.

Are you telling your customers when it's time for them to update what they have or to repeat the service they previously bought from you? As with the spice container ad, try persuading them to buy again by giving useful information on when they should repeat or replace your wares.

+ An attorney could send out a newsletter listing the six life changes that make it imperative to create a new will.

- ✦ A network security company could create a recommended checkup schedule according to specific risk factors.

- ✦ A car dealer could contact owners of four-year-old cars about safety and mileage improvements in this year's models.

On the Web

Read an article with further ideas and examples of contacting lost customers:

www.yudkin.com/lostcustomers.htm

Facilitate Delayed Purchases

For several months I've been thinking of signing up for..."
"I've read everything at your web site and now I'm ready to..."

From an email message and a telephone call received this week, these snippets indicate a common dynamic where customers make considered purchases rather than impulse buys.

Out of sight, people gather information and think through what they need. Finally they get in touch, ready to act.

To help this dynamic along:

+ Make yourself memorable and easy to find. An easy-to-remember business name, Google and Yellow Pages listings, "Contact Us" links at your web site all help in this regard. You certainly don't want customers to decide to buy and easily find only your competitors.

+ Stay in frequent contact with your universe of potential customers. This might mean regular advertisements, a weekly newsletter or follow-up calls to those who have requested information.

✦ Ask those who come out of the woodwork what triggered them to get moving. Incorporate ideas from their answers into your marketing copy to shorten others' time from thinking about hiring you to doing it.

Action Steps

✦ Brainstorm at least five ways you can encourage those who are considering a purchase to sign up or put down money earlier than they might otherwise do so. Implement the best one or two ideas that come up.

✦ Assess the extent of the pre-purchase information you provide at your web site and elsewhere. Think of what you can do to double and then continue to add such information, giving people more reasons to return to your site and finally buy.

Part 6
Planning Marketing Wisely

Time to Let Go?

A t the end of the calendar year, you probably reflect on how the year went and consider the blank slate that follows January 1.

When you think about marketing plans for the coming year, your mind naturally ponders what to do that's new or different.

Also weigh what to do less, what to stop doing.

+ Which activities no longer bring in business?

+ What routine takes so much energy you can't even think about planning something new?

+ Which effort brings you clients who make you groan?

+ What "to-do" makes you weary or annoyed just thinking of it?

+ Which creative task used to be fun but now feels like a chore?

Many of us continue doing what we've long done eons longer than we should.

Stopping frees up energy you can devote to learning, to trying something new or to sitting back and enjoying what you've achieved.

If you dare not stop, can you delegate a task to someone else on staff or to a freelancer?

If you dare not stop, can you change what's worn out its welcome so you feel good about it again?

Action Steps

+ Catalog your biggest energy drains, both personally and at work. One by one, determine whether it's best to eliminate it, delegate it or change it so it drains you less. Then review the list of remaining drains to make sure they'll be at a more tolerable level after you implement your plan for energy drains.

+ Rate yourself from 0 (clueless) to 5 (very certain) on how sure you are about which marketing activities do and don't bring in business. If you're less than a 3, read the chapter "Track Your Sales" later in this section and implement better—or some—customer tracking.

Strategic Opportunity Questions

At year's end, lots of folks sit down and set business and personal goals for the next calendar year. Before you do so, or instead, play around with some powerful questions, from Art Turock's book, *Invent Business Opportunities No One Else Can Imagine*:

+ What service would your customers ideally like to have, but would never request because they don't believe you can provide it?

+ How can you design your customer contacts to remove every shred of aggravation?

+ What are the conventional rules for success in your industry? If you broke the rules and did just the opposite, what opportunities might open up?

+ What value offering, such as operations excellence, customization of a service, or product innovation, could you develop to such a level of superiority that you could practically "customer-proof" your key accounts?

✦ What are the new services your leading-edge customers are starting to request?

✦ What accomplishment or result do you believe is extremely difficult or impossible to accomplish now, but if it could be done, would most powerfully increase your company's long-term profitability?

Strategic genius comes from such questions.

On the Web

Extend your thinking about options for your business by reading my article on 21 ways to earn more while working less:

www.marketingformore.com/21ways.htm

A Plan Cuts Suffering

Years ago, psychologist Neil Fiore led a support group for graduate students making little or no progress on their dissertations.

To his surprise, these strugglers worked many more hours than those who finished their writing projects on time. The strugglers put friends, recreation and enjoyment on hold. They suffered, constantly busy without accomplishing much.

The successful students worked, but only up to a point. Then they played. By not waiting to play until they'd finished their years-long project, Fiore points out, they felt better, stayed on track and got more done.

While a 200+ page dissertation can seem endless, marketing has no finish line at all. No wonder so many business people work and work at it without feeling they're getting anywhere.

A marketing plan structures your efforts. It lays out what to do and what not to do, then lets you put your energy elsewhere with a clear conscience.

Feeling overwhelmed? Create a clear, limited list of which tasks to do when. That's really all a marketing plan is.

With a realistic plan, you have less frazzle and less fizzle.

Action Steps

✦ Looking only at the coming month, formulate a marketing goal, such as: increase ezine subscribers, bid on more projects, sell more high-priced packages and so on. Then list tasks to perform that can take you to that goal along with how you'll measure success in reaching your goal. Make sure your list of tasks is doable, and if it is, voilà, you have a simple marketing plan.

✦ Repeat the process described just above while thinking about a quarter, six months or a year rather than just a month.

Plan Positively

When clients come to me for a marketing plan, their motivation is usually dissatisfaction: They're disappointed with their bottom line or market share, or they haven't been doing what they "should" to bring in new business.

Most of us change habits more easily with a clear, positive vision of what we'd like to achieve. Where business is concerned, that might be a revenue target, a lifestyle goal (longer vacations, more free time for family) or breaking into the big time (getting published, winning an award).

For example, in 2006 I decided to begin creating home-study courses so my husband and I could take a three-month road trip to Alaska, with income remaining steady. We did just that in the fall of 2007.

Another powerful yet little-used technique to focus your efforts is envisioning who you want as ideal clients.

By aligning your marketing strategy and wording to attract them, you can make that happen.

When planning, be sure also to congratulate yourself for what you've been doing well. Often that contains clues indicating how you move ahead with ease.

Action Steps

✦ Of the classic strategy categories of strengths, weaknesses, opportunities and threats, think particularly about your own strengths and opportunities and others' weaknesses and threats that you don't share. What options, ideas and possibilities do those concepts reveal?

✦ Imagine being commanded from on high to "Think Bold." Formulate a bold goal that goes beyond what feels comfortable. Envision reaching the goal and decide whether you want to commit yourself and others who'd need to be involved to the idea of getting there.

Assessing the Future

In 2001, many of us were blindsided by events that pulverized our business planning. The book *20/20 Foresight: Crafting Strategy in an Uncertain World* by Hugh Courtney offers a four-part framework that helps you assess your risks for the year ahead.

1. Are you relatively sure about what's ahead while unsure of its precise dimensions? When McDonald's scouts for a new site, its research predicts successful locations, though not exact revenues.

2. Are there a fixed number of alternative outcomes, though you don't know which will occur? When a bill affecting your industry's future is slated for legislative approval, the possibilities may consist of just "pass" or "not pass."

3. Can you define a wide range of possibilities? Although you wouldn't know how many of your current customers

would want your new add-on service, you might be able to nail the number as between X and Y percent.

4. Do you truly know nothing about your future success or challenges? This last scenario occurs rarely, Courtney argues. By identifying what makes the coming year uncertain, you can better prepare—and even relax.

Action Step

+ Identify your biggest concern about the future. What is the most likely scenario, and how could you prepare to cope with it? What is the least likely scenario, and how could you gear up to cope with that? Now decide what your most prudent course of action might be, then a somewhat riskier approach. Gather relevant information about the options. Trust your gut feeling about which way to go.

Consult Your Crystal Ball

Futurists charge corporate clients tens of thousands of dollars to project what might happen in their business environment in years to come. Yet anyone can learn to become a trend spotter and capitalize on new product or service opportunities, or the chance to sell to an untapped market.

+ Watch early adopters. If you have friends who always buy the latest gizmo or a teenager who leads the pack, observe what they get most excited about.

+ Track new laws. Reason your way to new tools and assistance that folks will need to comply.

+ Listen and ask. What new complaints do you hear in daily conversations? What weird questions are coming in on your email or to your company receptionist?

+ Notice unexpected customers. Are you getting orders from surprising locations or demographic groups?

This might indicate the need for an innovative marketing effort.

+ Note coincidences. When some particular surprise pops up twice in one week, it often indicates a trend. Stay alert and you may detect more examples of a phenomenon that you can take advantage of.

Don't get blindsided by change. Develop your own crystal ball!

Action Steps

+ Create a trend notebook or computer file in which you store observations, news and questions about trends. Review it periodically to spark realizations.

+ Put to work trends that you've noticed by issuing press releases and devising promotions around them.

+ At the end of a calendar year, issue predictions based on your observations, writing about them in press releases, ads or your blog.

Some Campaigns Last and Last

L ast month I stopped turning the pages of a comic book my thirteen-year-old goddaughter had brought to a family dinner. I pointed at an ad featuring Charles Atlas for a product that transforms 90-pound weaklings who get sand kicked in their faces.

"They had those ads in my childhood," I exclaimed. "Only now you can get the details at www dot-something dot-com."

My mother looked over my shoulder. "When I was growing up, we had those ads too."

This déjà vu repeated a few days later when I spotted a full-page ad in *Inc.* magazine spotlighting Smokey Bear and the slogan, "Only you can prevent forest fires"–another campaign that's been around as long as I can remember, updated with www.smokeybear.com.

Remember these examples when you assume you have to scrap your marketing materials and start over. Too often lately I've seen web sites I was going to recommend suddenly become bland and homogenized, without a trace of their former charm. Some marketing concepts, if you let them, keep on working, and working, and working.

Action Steps

+ Whenever you're on the verge of tossing out something that you're tired of, stop. Remind yourself that companies get bored with promotional ideas and branding far sooner than the public does. Before jettisoning a campaign or marketing identity, try just freshening it with a different angle or new details.

+ Look back at marketing materials you were using five, 10 and even 20 years ago. Do you see something you can bring back, either intact or tweaked so it feels timely and appropriate? If so, get going on it without delay.

Track Your Sales

We distribute a quarterly newsletter, exhibit at three trade shows a year, have two web sites and advertise in specialized magazines. How can we tell which marketing efforts (if any) are working and which not?"

The company from which this question came has a steady income, so some of its marketing efforts do work. To learn which ones is fairly simple, though it takes a bit of discipline.

First, it's surprisingly useful to ask each first-time buyer how they heard of you. Ask repeat customers what prompted them to call now. You can place clipboards next to the phones with columns for checking off the response. For orders coming in through email or the web, send back an email with this query.

Second, run offers with a bonus or discount if people use a certain code word. Assign a different code to different marketing vehicles and you'll soon know who's responding to which promotion.

Sometimes people don't remember where they heard of you, or they name a medium (like TV) that you've never used. But usually responses reveal how to market more intelligently in the future.

On the Web

Read more about simple tracking methods that don't require any math higher than simple counting:

www.marketingformore.com/simpletracking.htm

Establish Benchmarks

When those of us in the Northern Hemisphere begin to put away our beach towels, business minds turn to fresh beginnings. Before you implement marketing improvements, however, know what results you're getting from current efforts. Chances are, you're overlooking one or more of these crucial benchmarks:

+ How do customers generally find you—from your ads, through word of mouth, via Google searches? Answer this via a simple new-customer questionnaire or a survey.

+ What percentage of people who call or email with questions or request a quote, meeting or proposal turn into clients?

+ How much growth do you need to reach capacity? This applies to a professional practice, a health club or a subscription series, which can't grow beyond a certain point without adding more space, events or personnel.

+ What's the average long-term value of each customer?
+ How much are you spending to bring in each new customer?

With data on the above issues, you may realize your real marketing challenge differs from what you thought. Or you may spot tune-up opportunities costing a fraction of what you thought you'd need to invest.

Action Steps

+ Dislike numbers? Find someone on your staff or an outside assistant who is quantitatively inclined. Set them up with the numbers you want to track, the means to do so and the intervals (monthly, quarterly, etc.) at which you prefer to review reports.

+ Research averages on these benchmarks for your industry, so you can know whether you're exceeding or falling short of others' achievements. Generally reliable sources for such data are trade journals for your field and the relevant professional associations.

Prevent "Feast or Famine"

Careening from too much business to too little is not a healthy situation. Usually, overload causes a frenzied work pace, customer dissatisfaction and neglect of marketing. A sales shortfall prompts frantic flailing and equally counterproductive efforts to beat the bushes for projects.

Breaking this cycle requires creating business drivers that either work for you silently, week in and week out with little attention needed, or that you slot into your schedule and perform whether you feel you have time or not.

Marketing tactics that may cure feast or famine include:

+ A lead-generating ad that appears on a regular schedule
+ A newsletter (like *The Marketing Minute*) that likewise goes out whether you're busy or idle
+ Networking in your community so you're top of mind when needs arise

+ Web site content that's easily found and highly relevant to those suffering from the problem you solve
+ Automated messages to recent buyers that suggest related items or services
+ Consistent personal followup after completed projects to make sure clients were satisfied and to see if they have other needs

Get cracking on creating marketing consistency now!

On the Web

If you feel troubled by the feast-or-famine syndrome, listen to a coaching session in which I help a consultant understand the one-time tasks and routines he needed to create an effective marketing infrastructure for his business. It's a free downloadable audio just for readers of this book:

www.yudkin.com/infrastructure.htm

Low-volume Marketing Ideas

A *Marketing Minute* subscriber asked: "I sell a highly customized service and need only 12-15 clients a year. Most effective in drawing in new clients are recommendations from friends and clients. Do you have any other suggestions for marketing this type of low-volume business?"

I sure do:

+ A web site containing content that educates clients on the benefits and procedures of your service, including a FAQ page answering common questions of prospective clients

+ Publicity to magazines read by potential customers, which can not only spark interest but also channel interest toward you

+ Becoming active in organizations whose members, from your experience, are likely prospects for your service

- ✦ Invitingly offering to answer people's questions and going above and beyond in helping them, without pressuring them to buy
- ✦ Befriending professionals in a position to recommend your service
- ✦ Participation in online forums, discussion lists and member sites where enthusiasts for the type of thing you offer hang out
- ✦ Encouraging more referrals by staying in touch with past clients through chatty one-to-one emails, postcards and sent-through-the-mail notes

On the Web

Read comments from *Marketing Minute* subscribers on whether or not it's a good idea to offer motivating rewards for referrals:

www.yudkin.com/refpoll.htm

Do-It-Once Marketing

A little report called *The Myth of Passive Income* contains the consensus of 23 Internet marketers on the dream of turning your computer into a money mint, then spending your days drinking Mai-Tais by the pool or tooling around in your Maserati.

Nope, they say. "Passive income" requires work to create it and to support customers, make new deals and tweak what's working.

I agree. Even so, some marketing tactics you can do once and continue to enjoy their results for years.

High-impact, do-it-once marketing tactics include:

✦ Getting recommended by a government, magazine or university web site. Search engines rate such links as highly credible. A 2005 link from the magazine *Fast Company's* blog continues to bring dozens of visitors to my site every day.

✦ Issuing a keyword-rich press release, another credible move where search engines are concerned. One release I distributed last month launched me from no-wheresville to Google's #4 position.

✦ Posting articles for distribution by ezines and web-masters

✦ Posting content many colleagues decide to link to

✦ Tweaking your web pages to get noticed more easily by search engines

Action Steps

✦ List the do-it-once tasks from the list above that are appropriate for your business and schedule those activities some time during the next three months.

✦ Brainstorm other do-it-once tasks, such as weeding your product line or setting up a repeat contact system that practically runs itself, and slot those tasks into your schedule.

Your "By the Way" Assets

Successful people often reveal they discovered what rock-eted them to fortune by others saying, "You know, you're good at such-and-such. Can you teach me/help me?"

Beat them to it by highlighting and exploiting hard-to-name talents or unintended accomplishments. Ask yourself:

+ In what ways do I love going above and beyond, or deeper than others?
+ What kind of commentary of mine–in conversation, on my blog–seems to strike a nerve?
+ Which unexpected skills have I mastered to do what I do?
+ What data have I collected that others could use?

Ask customers:

+ What do you like about doing business with me that you don't experience elsewhere?
+ Looking back, what results from the work we did together seemed to come out of left field?

The answers may point to a lucrative sideline service or information product you can develop—or your next career.

For instance, maybe your B&B hospitality generates matches among guests or your sports coaching produces better posture.

Identify your "by the way" assets, bottle them for sale and enjoy the extra profits.

Action Steps

✦ Set up lunch meetings with colleagues or clients who know you well. Ask them, "If you were going to recommend a post-retirement career for me that uses my best talents or what I've learned from what I'm doing now, what would that be?" Pay special attention to suggestions that surprise you, yet feel plausible.

✦ Sit down with a pile of client files and flip through them slowly in search of concepts you could easily and enjoyably teach in seminars or information products.

Do People Shop for What You Sell?

A re people actively hunting–shopping–for your products or services, or do they generally buy after an unplanned encounter with you, your facility or your marketing materials?

Hardly anyone hires a plumber because they spot his truck and decide to get their toilet fixed. Rather, they have a plumbing problem and if they don't already know a plumber or can't get a personal recommendation, they send their fingers walking through the Yellow Pages.

Online, ads in search engines (such as Google or Bing) can cost-effectively capture the attention of folks shopping online for something they know they need. However, search engine ads are as powerless as the Yellow Pages to reach buyers who aren't hunting for what you sell and who may not even realize that offerings like yours exist.

Media coverage, public speaking, networking, affiliate promotions and links from informational web sites to yours can get someone interested in buying something they had not been thinking about and perhaps had not ever heard of.

Don't use a marketing wrench for the job of a screwdriver. (You may need both!)

Action Steps

+ List your major products and services, and rate each one from 1 to 5 according to whether it's rarely shopped for (1) or nearly always shopped for (5). For a score of 4 or 5, make sure you are investing money and energy in search engine marketing and directories. For a score of 1 or 2, forget about those shopping-oriented tools. In between, aim at a mix of efforts.

+ For items rarely shopped for, survey those who bought from you about the media they pay most attention to (radio, TV, web sites, blogs, publications), entertainment venues they patronize, leisure pursuits they enjoy, and so on, with the idea of learning where and how you can best come across their paths.

Part 7
Bound for Profit

Constraints Can Help

You'd think that someone who'd started a company once on the cheap would do even better the second time with a budget several times larger. In fact, having additional cash to throw around hardly ever leads to proportionately better results for second timers. More money may trigger less creativity and spending on ego expenses rather than what lures customers.

Chris Yeh, Chief Marketing Officer for TargetFirst, conducted an experiment along these lines. One team received a healthy marketing budget for launching a new product. The second team received the same objective but no budget to speak of.

"The traditional team did a great job of planning an opt-in email campaign that ran to our target audience," he says. "The $1 team uncovered barter opportunities, undiscovered advertisers, and obscure but scrappy distribution partners.

Though both teams were successful, the $1 team produced double the revenue and customers at basically zero cash cost."

So next time you're tempted to complain that you don't have enough money to market, get your ingenuity in gear. Think. Make do. Constraints help creativity—it's proven!

Action Steps

+ Before requesting a nice-sized budget, imagine that you have to reach your marketing goal with only $100 to spend. How could you exploit that budget to the fullest?

+ Imagine now a constraint of time—you must reach your goal with only five hours of work by you or anyone else. How does that get your imagination whirring?

+ Now suppose you had to create maximum impact with just a single marketing tactic. Which tactic would you choose and how would you handle this challenge?

+ Gather the insights from these thought experiments and determine how you can use them to ensure that the money, time and resources you do have get the greatest results.

How Much Does Marketing Cost?

Marketing costs money. But unlike what you spend on, say, tires or vacations, that money can come back to you many times over. So instead of fretting over marketing dollars going out, focus on return on investment.

Begin by knowing how much each new customer is worth to you. Simply divide your annual sales by the number of customers that year to determine how much each customer brings in, on average. If buyers tend to stick with you for years, their value correspondingly goes up. Finally, subtract your costs to arrive at your average profit per customer.

If each average new customer is worth, let's say, $5,000 in profit, then spending as much as $500 to bring him or her into your fold is not expensive, but rather a prudent investment.

Looked at another way, spending $3,000 on a marketing campaign that will probably bring in at least two new $5,000 customers is a very smart use of available cash.

In setting your marketing budget, don't be penny wise and pound foolish.

❧　❧

Action Steps

+ Calculate the average value of a customer, using the procedure described above. Then for any marketing campaign designed to attract new customers, multiply that average value times the number of new customers you can reasonably expect to gain from the campaign, then subtract the cost of the campaign. If your mathematical result is a positive number, proceed with the campaign. If it's a high positive number, go ahead with gusto!

+ Hire an intern who is studying business in college and has a good head for numbers to go through your sales records and compare the return on investment of marketing initiatives and methods you used in the previous year. Adjust your spending accordingly.

Raise Prices Simply

If I had snake-oil ambitions, I'd create a five-step process for successfully raising prices. First, work up elaborate reasons for the rise and sprinkle in heartfelt apologies. Express hope that clients will forgive you for this audacious step. Then oh so gingerly lay the foundation for your news, and so on.

This report would sell.

I know that because when I tell clients who are teetering from unprofitability how actually to raise their fees, they do not want to believe me.

What's best: Make a simple, factual statement, like "As of September 1, our fees will be $2,250 for Service A and $3,870 for Service B." No explanation, no apology. Then go on to the next item of business. That's it!

Unless you're a public utility, you don't owe customers information about how you arrive at prices or why you run your business as you do. Apologies for prices position you as subservient to clients, rather than equal. Apologies also invite opinions and objections rather than the acceptance that follows the factual announcement 99 times out of a hundred.

On the Web

Of 355 *Marketing Minute* subscribers who responded to a survey I ran, 29 percent named "My clients can't afford to pay that much" as the main reason their income wasn't going through the roof. Read my critical commentary on that belief in a free report you can download at:

www.marketingformore.com/survey.htm

From Free to Fee

Week after week I send out my thoughts on marketing for free. Why bother? With the *Marketing Minute*, my articles posted online and talks to business groups, I've seen "free" become the passageway to "fee."

When a consultant asked if she should give away perspectives and ideas in her newsletter, I replied, "The more you give away, the more they understand why they need to hire you."

Direct marketer Bob Serling disagrees. "Through many years of trial and error, I've discovered that making a sale on the first try should always be your primary goal. Accordingly, I recommend you rarely give anything away as a lead generator, especially on the Internet."

Serling continues, "Without some type of commitment on the prospect's part, you don't really have the beginning of a relationship. Worse, by continuing to give more and more away, you're conditioning prospects not to buy–but to expect even more for free."

When I polled *Marketing Minute* subscribers on this issue, 68 percent agreed with giving away free bait, 9 percent took the opposite view (most "reluctantly") and 23 percent responded with a mixed opinion.

On the Web

Read the opinions and explanations given by *Marketing Minute* subscribers on the question of whether or not "free" leads to "fee":

www.yudkin.com/freeorfee.htm

Why Would They Pay?

A client in the startup phase of his business was troubled by a web site offering at no cost the service he was planning to charge for. "I don't see why anyone would pay for something they can get free," he said.

Here are a few reasons:

✦ You provide a more convenient interface or more options.

✦ They don't know about the no-cost service.

✦ You provide information in a more organized, tangible format they can keep on their shelf.

✦ They'd rather patronize an expert than a no-name service.

✦ They prefer a no-ads experience.

✦ You offer camaraderie or support along with the service.

✦ Your site is more entertaining, more sophisticated or more no-nonsense.

✦ They trust companies that charge and mistrust those that don't.

✦ They like what you offer and buy without shopping for another provider.

✦ You were recommended by a source they trust.

✦ You're local to them and they prefer to support local companies.

✦ You support a charity they also support.

Assuming everyone shops and makes buying decisions the same way is a huge mistake.

Action Steps

✦ Catalog the items you yourself pay for that are available free in some other format, such as bottled water, the newspaper delivered to your home, books that you could borrow at the library, software that has a free version and so on. Articulate the reasons you do so, and reflect on the lessons that emerge.

✦ Brainstorm at least ten more reasons someone might pay for a paid version of what others offer free. If you compete head to head with a free option, identify which of these reasons and the ones listed above apply to your situation, and craft your marketing pitch accordingly.

You Can Charge for Meetings

Do you hate meetings? *Newsweek* profiled a guy named Derik Rawson who had the nerve to act on his antipathy.

A web designer who had hated meetings throughout 15 years in the film business, he tells clients he charges $125 an hour—unless they require his presence at meetings, in which instance his fee doubles. His clients either pay up, learn to live without meetings or take their business elsewhere.

Likewise, inspired by two other marketing consultants who decline "get-to-know-you" meetings and who charge for "pick-your-brains" lunch meetings, a couple of years back I began telling clients that if they had questions about me, I'd be happy to answer them over the phone and provide references, but for all in-person meetings I charge my regular hourly rate.

"It would be a working session," I explain. "You get my consulting expertise and finish the meeting with new insights." Serious new clients understood and paid.

Emphasize the value you provide, and you might pull this off, too.

Action Steps

✦ Before putting this strategy into practice, role-play with a friend or two what you'll say if someone thinks you're crazy to charge for a first client meeting. Instruct your role-playing partner to object strenuously to your proposal. Then rehearse your best ways to respond.

✦ Setting aside your own feelings, write up an explanation of why it's beneficial to your client to pay for an initial meeting.

Perceived Value Requires a Price

Governor Deval Patrick's proposal to eliminate tuition for Massachusetts community colleges recently received a thoughtful response from the president of Greenfield Community College, Robert Pura.

"We want to really deeply explore what the word 'free' means and conjures up" before we implement such a proposal, Pura said, suggesting that increasing financial aid might be a better way to make college more affordable.

For state residents, the effective cost might be the same with both proposals, but "free tuition" might encourage "a wave of students who take their education lightly, over-enroll and drop classes without much thought," Pura told the *Daily Hampshire Gazette*. Beefing up financial aid communicates responsibility rather than entitlement and may encourage a more serious approach to education.

Likewise, business coach Mark Silver says an acupuncturist he worked with found her patients getting well faster when she raised her fees. Apparently when they were paying more, patients were more likely to do as she suggested between sessions, to get their money's worth.

Because prices influence perceived value, prices also affect client behavior and their results.

Action Steps

+ Reflect on the value you'd like customers to perceive for what you sell. Then contemplate whether or not your pricing fits with and promotes that perceived value.

+ Consider the pros and cons of raising your prices but offering a limited number of "scholarships" for particular reasons.

Protect Your Marketing

When you've invested time and resources into creating promotional material and content that bring you business, you sure don't want a perfect stranger piggybacking off your efforts by appropriating your work.

I've identified online plagiarizers by plunking a distinctive phrase from material I want to remain exclusive into Google to see who has copied those words. But the other day I used a much easier way to catch word thieves: www.copyscape.com.

This terrific no-cost tool locates other web pages substantially similar to a specific page of yours.

Normally a polite email to an infringer induces them to take down the plagiarized material. However, in one case where the thief refused, I used Copyscape on other pages of the site in question and discovered two other marketers whose work the thief had also stolen.

Together, the three of us will soon have this bandit begging for mercy.

When a polite request doesn't work, the next step is telling the offender's web hosting company about the infringement. Almost always, they act quickly to enforce their no-infringement terms of service.

Action Steps

✦ If you have particular web pages you strongly wish to protect, register them with your national copyright authority for a nominal fee. Find the relevant US information, forms and fees at www.copyright.gov, Canada's at cipo.gc.ca, the UK's at www.ipo.gov.uk, Australia's at www.copyright.org.au and New Zealand's at www.iponz.govt.nz.

✦ Learn about the procedures for reporting a violation to the culprit's web host by going to one of these web pages:

http://tinyurl.com/DCMAtakedown

http://tinyurl.com/DMCAnotice

What Tip Behavior Teaches

Think you know what propels your customers to decide what price is right? It could be the stars, world events—or the weather, according to an Associated Press report last week.

Michael Lynn, a Cornell University professor who has been studying tipping for 20 years, says that whether it's sunny or cloudy has as much influence on the size of a restaurant tip as the quality of service. In addition, although people claim they tip worse for poor service, they actually tip their usual percentage when displeased with their waiter and then just never go back.

Several lessons here apply to those of you not in the restaurant business.

First, don't assume people's buying behavior is within your control. Likewise, when orders suddenly slow, it may not be because of something you've done.

Second, don't believe what customers say about why they buy. They may not be conscious of their reasons.

Third, you might be annoying your clientele greatly even if you receive no complaints. Repeat patronage and people sending over their friends and colleagues are surer signs that you're serving well.

Action Step

+ Turn a randomly selected month's sales into a chart showing either the number or the amount of sales, day by day. Notice the degree of variation. Resolve not to get concerned about a drop in sales unless you see a much more dramatic drop than shown on the chart or the drop persists, in a pattern that can't be explained by the news, your promotions, holidays or other external factors.

Recommended Books

The following books provide valuable insights into the aspects of marketing covered in *Marketing Strategy.*

Abraham, Jay, *The Sticking Point Solution: 9 Ways to Move Your Business from Stagnation to Stunning Growth in Tough Economic Times.* New York: Vanguard Press, 2009. Tips for achieving ever-growing profitability.

Kennedy, Dan S., *How to Make Millions With Your Ideas.* New York: Plume, 1996. Starting with just an idea? This book explains the moves that can turn it into a thriving business.

Levinson, Jay Conrad, *Guerrilla Marketing Excellence: The Fifty Golden Rules for Small-Business Success.* Boston: Houghton Mifflin, 1993. Explores the thinking necessary for cost-effective, satisfying business success.

Maister, David H. et al, *The Trusted Advisor.* New York: Touchstone, 2000. How to earn the trust of clients and use it to build a thriving professional practice.

Shepherd, David, *Your Business or Your Life: 8 Steps for Getting All You Want Out of Both.* Austin, TX: Balios Publishing, 2001. If you're frustrated at building the business that most suits you, read this one.

Stanny, Barbara, *Secrets of Six-Figure Women: Surprising Strategies to Up Your Earnings and Change Your Life.* New York: HarperBusiness, 2002. Based on interviews with over 150 diverse high-earning women, explains the mindset needed for success that fits your values and provides the lifestyle you want.

Weiss, Alan, *Million Dollar Consulting: The Professional's Guide to Growing a Practice,* 4th edition. New York: McGraw-Hill, 2009. Very smart advice, grounded in experience, for steering a consulting business.

Get the Whole Series!

What you are reading is the third of five volumes collecting my *Marketing Minute* columns and presenting them by theme. The other volumes are:

✦ Book 1: *Persuading People to Buy: Insights on Marketing Psychology That Pay Off for Your Company, Professional Practice or Nonprofit Organization*

✦ Book 2: *Meatier Marketing Copy: Insights on Copywriting That Generates Leads and Sparks Sales*

✦ Book 4: *Publicity Tactics: Insights on Creating Lucrative Media Buzz*

✦ Book 5: *The Marketing Attitude: Insights That Help You Build a Worthy Business*

The series includes two audio CDs for each volume, on which I read the columns in that book. Listening to the contents in your car or while exercising often triggers ideas you'll want to implement in your company, professional practice or nonprofit organization.

For more information or to purchase the rest of the Marketing Insight Guides, go to:

www.marketinginsightguides.com.

If you're not already a subscriber, sign up to receive the *Marketing Minute* free in your inbox every Wednesday by going to www.yudkin.com/markmin.htm.

Index

About the Author

Since 1981, when she launched her writing career by successfully pitching her first freelance article to editors at the *New York Times,* Marcia Yudkin has steered her business in fruitful directions.

Prior to the books in the Marketing Insight Guides series, she published 11 books, including *Freelance Writing for Magazines and Newspapers,* a Book-of-the-Month Club selection, and *6 Steps to Free Publicity,* now in its third edition.

Her "Marketing Minute" segment aired weekly throughout New England for more than a year on WABU TV, and it turned into a free weekly newsletter on creative marketing and publicity that reaches more than 12,000 loyal subscribers from all around the world.

Marcia Yudkin serves as a marketing mentor and advises business owners, independent professionals and corporate marketers on smart moves for their ventures. Clients include publishers, professional associations, software companies, consultants, online merchants and seminar promoters, among others.

She has a Ph.D. degree from Cornell University and a B.A. from Brown University.

For More Information

Main web site: www.yudkin.com

Subscribe to the *Marketing Minute*:

    www.yudkin.com/markmin.htm

Mentoring program: www.marketingformore.com

Publicity services: www.pressreleasehelp.com

Contact Marcia Yudkin: marcia@yudkin.com

Breinigsville, PA USA
04 October 2010
246636BV00001B/1/P